D1342829

Hamlyn

London · New York · Sydney · Toronto

How to play
Darts
Dave Whitcombe

Acknowledgements

The sequence photographs were photographed by Don Morley of All-Sport at the Central Ward Residents Club at Morden, Surrey. Additional photographs were supplied by Duncan Raban of All-Sport and by *Darts World* magazine. The cover picture was supplied by *Radio Times*. The rules in Chapter Fourteen are reproduced by kind permission of the British Darts Organisation. To all the above, the author and Publishers extend their thanks.

cover : Eric Bristow
front endpaper : The home of most of today's darts – the public house
title spread : Tony Brown
back endpaper : The 1980 Winmau World Masters: John Lowe, on the oche, playing Jocky Wilson

LEABHARLANNA ATHA CLIATH
HENRY STREET LIBRARY
ACC. NO.   0600 346587
COPY NO.   CC 1004
INV. NO.   1616
PRICE IR£   3.72
CLASS   794.3

Published by
The Hamlyn Publishing Group Limited
London · New York · Sydney · Toronto
Astronaut House, Feltham, Middlesex, England

© Copyright The Hamlyn Publishing Group Limited 1981

ISBN 0 600 34658 7

All rights reserved. No part of this publication may be reproduced, stored in a retrieval system, or transmitted, in any form or by any means, electronic, mechanical, photocopying, recording or otherwise, without the permission of The Hamlyn Publishing Group Limited

Printed in Italy

Contents

Chapter One
The Old Game

Opposite: Most people's idea of the game of darts – a friendly game in the local pub.

As most people know, darts has been played for hundreds of years. We know that it was played in Ireland in the 16th century and we also know that it was played, according to the history books, aboard the *Mayflower* by the Pilgrim Fathers in 1620. Apart from these well known facts it is very difficult to obtain much more information about the origins of the game.

It is also true to say that nobody knows how the numbers on the dartboard originated. I suppose it is quite reasonable to assume that our modern day game is a simple progression from the medieval days, when our forefathers used to throw foot long arrows at a log end to test their skill. These arrows were used in battle at close-quarters and were heavily weighted at one end.

Over a long period of time the game slowly progressed towards its present state and different variations were adopted. It was not until the 20th century that the first all-metal barrel was made and not until about the mid-1930s that one could actually buy a *set* of darts, as before they had only been sold singly.

It was in the 1930s, 1940s and 1950s that now famous names started to emerge. When the legendary Jim Pike, Joe Hitchcock and Tommy Barrett used to play, they could not have realised that they would come to be looked upon as the first real stars of our great sport today.

I believe, and I think most people will agree with me, that the game of darts really began when players of the above calibre took to the sport, and helped to make it the most popular of indoor games. There is also no doubt in my mind that these players had as many skills on the board as our top stars of today. The fact that they used antiquated darts, by today's standards, did not make any difference at all. They still scored 100s, 140s and 180s as do the players today. They also used to play on a 9-ft throw, which is much longer than the present day 7 ft 9¼ in.

Of course, the game in its present form has improved by leaps and bounds. The equipment is now much more varied, i.e. there are hundreds of different types of barrels to choose from, many variations of flights and stems etc., and the actual dartboards themselves have improved greatly. We must bear in mind that there were never any big open competitions with large cash prizes like there are today, and that most players only played for fun. The competition between players was also smaller as in effect there was no ladder to climb. But all in all let us not forget the players of yesteryear, for they were still great players and most important, the pioneers of the modern game of darts.

Chapter Two
The New Game

In 1966 the Greater London Super League was formed. It was set up to enable the better teams in various leagues to participate so as to make worthy opposition for each other. As the years went by, more teams joined and the standard has risen so much that in my opinion this is the best super league in the world. Every team in this league is without question a good one. Unlike many local leagues where usually one or two teams dominate the scene and win all the cups, there is nothing certain in this particular super league.

In the 1970s we saw the very first inter-county games get under way. Players were selected from the best around in their area, and home and away matches were arranged. The games were played under rules drawn up by the British Darts Organisation. The men's games were twelve-a-side to be played individually, the best of 3 legs 501. The ladies played four-a-side as a team the best of 3 legs. There was an 'A' and 'B' team for both men and women.

The games have somewhat changed over the years and now we see the men's 'A' team play the best of 5 legs 501 and the ladies

Darts at the top level. An international match between Scotland and Wales in 1981.

now play individual games like the men except that it is played five-a-side, the best of 3 legs 501.

With the coming of the inter-county games we saw various Open Tournaments get under way so as to enable players to compete for cash prizes. These competitions proved very popular and more and more were arranged. It was in the 1970s that we also witnessed the coming about of international matches.

People who gained a reputation in county games and who played consistently well were selected to represent their country, and from those very few came the professional players of today. One does not have to play for one's country to be a professional, but prestige-wise it certainly helps to establish oneself as a top player.

There is now a lot of television coverage on major events and over the last ten years we have seen many companies becoming interested in sponsorship. Thousands of pounds are being given away each year in prize money and more tournaments are being held. The spectrum is now worldwide and many countries compete. National newspapers report regularly on major events and there are now papers and magazines solely about darts.

I have entitled this chapter 'The New Game' because I wanted to say a little about how the game has progressed from the very early days. It is now getting more and more popular as each season goes by, and I am sure that one day we will see a professional circuit with very large prize money as in golf and tennis today.

Chapter Three
The Beginning for Me

Like many boys at Secondary School who have only a short time left before they leave, I found my days were not very happy. I do not really want to criticise the Secondary Boys School, but apart from teaching me to read, write and add two and two, it taught me little else! So when I was in my last year all I wanted to do was find a job ready for when I eventually left. Alas though, my Headmaster had other ideas and the fourth formers who, like myself, did not intend staying on, were made to suffer lectures from various people on different careers. Those who had shown skills with their hands in either metalwork or woodwork were given many interesting talks on putting their talents to good use in Chatham Dockyard and advised to train as apprentices in some field or other. Myself and a few others who did not show any skills at all were given extremely interesting lectures on the Army, Navy and Air Force. Well I am glad to say that I did not take any of these talks seriously and decided to find my own job.

I left school at the earliest opportunity, when I was 15 years of age and within a month I was indentured as an apprentice electrician. Over the next three years I had little time for anything other than work and would do as much overtime as possible. However, when I was 18 years old I started to have a little light refreshment in the local pub at dinner times. A few of the older men would have a game of darts to pass the time and after watching them having a great amount of fun, I felt I wanted to join in. I seemed to be always on the chalks and after a few weeks of continually losing, I began to blame the pub darts. So one night after work I went to the nearest sports shop and bought myself a set of darts. 'Now let's see if they can beat me,' I thought to myself. But after a few more weeks on the chalks, I decided that just to have your own set of darts was not enough. Practice was the word and so my friend Mike Fellingham and I used to go out many an evening for jollification and a few games of darts.

After some time I was able to hold my own with the lads at work and soon winning as many as I was losing. My interest grew stronger and I decided to join a team at my local, 'The Old Lord Raglan' in Chatham. I still was not very good, but neither were they, so they were glad to have me! I fitted in quite well and enjoyed myself very much.

After about a year I knew that I was getting quite useful and the captain decided that I should represent the team in the annual league knock-out singles event. I tried to prepare myself for this by putting in many hours of practice but was not very confident as I stepped up to play my opponents. After a few scrapes though, and a bit of luck, I found myself in the final and was to face a very experienced player who had been playing since I was in nappies. It proved to be a very close game but in the third and decisive leg I got to a double first and was looking down the barrel of my dart into double 16. My first dart missed but my second went in. I had won my first singles title – and I felt ten feet tall on presentation night when I went to collect my trophy.

From this time on, I was really hooked and I would practise during any spare time I had. I joined other teams and played about four times a week. I began to compete in open competitions and it was in fact the first one I entered that set me on the road to being a professional player. At this time I was 21 years old and mixed with a few of the best players around. One of them proved to be a very good friend to me as time went by. His name is Tony Love, but he is better known to his friends as 'Chic'. I do not quite know how he got this nickname and he himself cannot remember. He was at one time quite an exceptional player and in fact was Kent's first international. He also represented Great Britain in the U.S.A. in 1974. Although he has now slightly lost his edge, he still maintains a place in the Kent County 'A' side quite comfortably. It was Chic who entered me in my first open and we both went along to try our luck.

The name of the tournament was the 'Surrey Open' and it was to be held in Kingston upon Thames. We arrived to find many of

The Winmau World Masters 1980, and this is me collecting my cheque and souvenir.

the top stars there. Chic fared well to get into the last 32 but I was playing a little better and found myself in the last 8. I was now to face the supreme test; whether or not I could play under pressure, because I was to meet one of the world's best in the shape of Eric Bristow. The game was up and down but I found I was more consistent. I scraped through to win 2–1 only to find that I had another task on my hands in the form of Leighton Rees. He was undoubtedly the world's best at the time so I just hoped for a miracle. My prayers were answered in that Leighton played below par and I was through to the final. My opponent was none other than Alan Glazier, another world class player who a week beforehand had narrowly lost in the final of the British Open. After an exceptional bit of luck when Alan missed his doubles I found myself the winner and almost fainted as I realised what I had achieved in only my first open competition. This was definitely 'it' for me and a few weeks later I signed for Kent and was given a chance in the 'B' side. I was progressing by strides and entering many tournaments all over the country. I did not win them all and indeed it never entered my head that I would. Nevertheless, I kept trying and had my fair share of successes. Over the next few years I steadily progressed and finally reached one of my goals, to be selected to play for my country, and I can proudly say that I still hold a place in the England side.

To progress from playing in a bottom of the league team in a local division to playing for the greatest dart team on earth is one of the greatest satisfactions that I have ever known. Another honour which is a great one in its own right was to be selected as Captain of Kent, the county team for which I play, in the Inter-

My excitement at winning my first major tournament, the Marlboro Masters in 1980, and the calmer pleasure that follows as I collect the handsome trophy and the cheque from the sponsors.

County League. The selection came somewhat as a surprise as we have many great players in the team, as do many county sides. Anyway, I am very proud of this honour and am somewhat boastful of it, I'm afraid.

I mentioned earlier that England is the greatest dart team on earth. Well, without any disrespect to, say, Wales, Scotland or the U.S.A., England reigns supreme. In a fifteen-a-side men's match and five-a-side ladies' match, England are undoubtedly the strongest. Perhaps in a three- or four-man event where many countries compete, for instance the World Cup, a team which can click together might be on par with England. But I personally feel that it will be many years before other countries can match England in strength.

Obviously, many people would dearly love to play for their country and although everyone cannot do so, I wish anyone who has their heart set on it the very best of luck. For my part now, I hope to progress from playing in the fifteen-man and ten-man teams in International matches and Home International matches respectively, to earning a place in the four- or three-man teams to play in the Europe Cup or World Cup or other such event where many countries compete.

As far as competitions go, until this book was written, I had yet to win a major title on my own. I had come close on many occasions, being in the last four of the British Open twice and getting in the last eight once, reaching the last eight of the British Gold Cup, the final stages of the North American Open and the Danish Open and losing in the final of the *News of the World*. I had had many successes at open tournaments though, winning the

Surrey Open three times in succession, the Suffolk Open, Essex Open, Langley Open, Butlins/Watneys Open two years in succession and many more. I had also won the British Open Pairs with Tony Sontag, my England colleague and great friend, on the first time we had entered this competition together. I could not really complain about my successes in tournaments but I did want to win a major title because having done so I thought it would then be possible to win more. The first one, I thought, would be the hardest!

I am glad to say that a week or two after delivering the manuscript of this book to the publisher, in December 1980, I at last won a major title: the Marlboro Masters, so all the verbs in the previous paragraph had to be changed to the past tense.

I will stop here as I cannot predict my future in darts and this rundown of my progress gives one route up the ladder. I would just like to say that if any of you think that you can make your way in darts, but are a little perturbed about playing at the bottom, do not worry. Just have patience, try hard and above all never give up. I started literally at the bottom and although as yet I am not at the top, I am only a few rungs short. Perhaps these are the hardest rungs to climb. I hope you have the enjoyment that I have had.

To show that it is not all winning, this is me on the way to defeat by Nicky Virachkul in the World Masters, despite the healthy state of the score.

Chapter Four
Various Boards

There are various types of dartboard in existence at the moment. The elm boards were very popular at one time and indeed are still used in some leagues and in one of the world's most coveted competitions, the *News of the World*.

This type of board, because of the amount of looking after it requires, is rarely used in competitions. When not in use it must be kept in water, otherwise it gets too dry and cracks and goes out of shape. In competitions, because of the number of boards required (for example the British Open normally uses a total of 64 boards over its three days) it would be ridiculous even to think of using elm boards. They have one advantage which is that they are reversible. The wire numbers merely have to be removed from one side and placed on the other.

Elm has now given way to bristle. These boards need virtually no looking after other than the fact that they must be turned

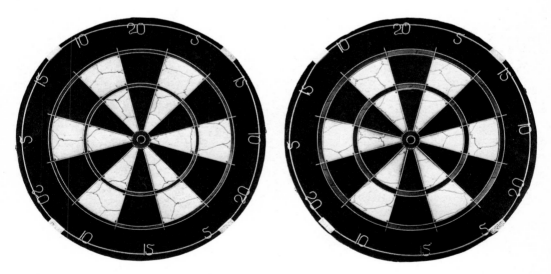

regularly. Due to the majority of players aiming for either treble 20 or 19, the amount of wear in just those two areas is tremendous, whether the board is used in a pub or for competition. Therefore the board must be turned at regular intervals so that all the segments receive an even amount of wear and tear. This is done by removing the numerals wire, turning the board until a treble space which has been hardly used appears in the treble 20 position, and replacing the wire. Because of the little attention they require, bristle boards are normally used in most major and minor competitions.

Two fives boards, a narrow fives board on the left and wide fives board on the right. Note the difference in the widths of the doubles and trebles.

17

There have been quite a few different boards used in various regions but only a handful have survived over the years. Take for instance the Club Board which was used before the war by the Club and Institute Union. This had a small 'bull' in each segment in place of the treble inner ring. Also the 'Tonbridge' board with the treble ring on the outside and a half diamond shape inside, counting double.

There are however, still in use today in certain parts of Kent and Yorkshire, the 'double' board which as the picture shows has no trebles. In parts of East London the fives board is very popular and although made of bristle the design of the board is totally different from either the 'double' or 'treble' board.

A selection of regional and little-used boards is illustrated. The most common board is the subject of the next chapter.

Various doubles boards. Top left is an Irish all-black board, and top right a board sometimes called a Lincoln or Medway board, which looks similar but is only 15 inches across its playing area. Bottom left is a Yorkshire or Kent 'doubles' board and bottom right a Burton board, in which the diamonds counted as 25.

18

Chapter Five
Approved Board

The 'treble' board is the most popular and is used all over the country. Indeed it is the only board many players have seen. It is divided into sections 1-20 but not in numerical order as the picture shows. It is more commonly known as the clock or London board. There is a bull in the centre which scores 50 and an outer bull which scores 25. Then come the trebles, doubles and singles from 20 downwards.

The throwing distance throughout Britain, and in fact throughout the world, has varied from time to time and place to place, and arguments arose when players were subjected to different throws in various tournaments.

Therefore the World Darts Federation got together and decided there should be just one distance for all super leagues, county leagues, international matches and major tournaments. They settled on 7 ft 9¼ in or 2·37 metres. This has made things easier all round but there are still some leagues whose habits die hard, and who still use an 8 ft throwing distance.

The standard dimensions of the approved board are as follows:
Double and treble rings, inside width measurement=8 mm ($\frac{5}{16}$ in)
Bull, inside diameter= 12·7 mm (0·5 in)
Semi-centre or outer bull, inside diameter =31 mm (1·25 in)
Outside edge of double wire to centre bull=170 mm (6·75 in)
Outside edge of treble wire to centre bull =117 mm (4·25 in)
Outside edge of double wire to outside edge of opposite double wire =342 mm (13·5 in)
Overall dartboard diameter =457 mm (18·0 in)
Spider wire gauge (minimum standard wire gauge)=16 SWG

The official B.D.O.-approved trebles board.

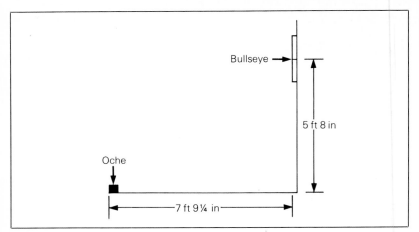

The illustration shows the standard dimensions of the throwing distance between oche and board. These will help if you decide to put a board up in your home.

The game itself is varied. The most popular is 501 straight start, but sometimes 301 is used with a double start and indeed this is the format for the very popular North American Open. However, in both games the players must finish on the correct double. The scores are subtracted from the starting figure.

A game of 501 is usually scored as shown in the table below.

You will see in the first leg Player A required 40 to go out so he would go for double 20. If he fails in his attempt to hit the double and scores a single twenty, he would then require double ten. Should he leave an odd number such as 5 he must then get a single 1 to leave double 2.

A player does not have to go for the most obvious double. Some professional players when requiring double 5 will go for a single 2 to leave double 4 – a much easier double than 5 because should he miss and get a single 4 he has two darts left at double 2.

A game of 301 double start is scored in exactly the same way as the game of 501 below except that a double must be achieved before scoring takes place.

Feet must be behind the oche, or an imaginary extension of it. The position at the top is legal, as both feet are completely behind the line of the oche. The positions centre and bottom are illegal.

Player A		Player B		Player A		Player B		Player A		Player B	
1st leg 501			501	2nd leg 501			501	3rd leg 501			501
*100	401	85	416	140	361	*100	401	* 60	441	81	420
81	320	95	321	60	301	100	301	125	316	85	335
125	195	100	221	99	202	60	241	100	216	45	290
85	110	60	161	65	137	140	101	60	156	100	190
70	40	125	36			101 Game		100	56	60	130
40 Game Shot						Shot		56 Game Shot			

Player A wins this match by 2 legs to 1.

*A coin is tossed for who throws first and the winner goes first in first and third legs. The loser goes first in the second leg.

Chapter Six
Equipment

Darts, Flights and Stems

When you set out to buy your first set of darts it is worth your
while to take time and consider what exactly you are going after.
Think about how you throw a dart: do you throw it hard or do
you throw it softly? Do you like a light or heavy dart? There are
many sports shops around which have a dartboard set up inside
and it would be in your own interest to find one of these, so that
you can try any darts you might consider buying.

There are many different weights and sizes of darts so have a
practice with them all. Try long barrels, short barrels, heavy darts,
light darts and ring the changes with regard to stems and flights.
The shopkeeper should not mind, especially if he thinks he has got
a sale. Consider the grip of the dart too. If you have hands that
tend to perspire, it is better to try darts with plenty of grip. If
your hands do not sweat you might prefer a smooth barrel.

Fortunately enough, darts are not very expensive, especially

when compared with the equipment used in other sports. If you
buy a set of darts and after a few weeks find that you are not
satisfied with them – for example, perhaps you feel an extra couple
of grams will improve your game – go and try another set. You
may be lucky enough to swop your darts with someone who thinks
that he may benefit from a lighter set. You may even be able to
resell them to someone who cannot afford to buy a new set.

Having finally decided on a set to suit you, look after them and
get used to them. They are your way to the top. I tried many
different sets until I settled with the 24-gram nickel tungstens that
I now use.

One point to bear in mind is that when taking part in matches,

The range of darts I
use and market, in
three different weights,
22 gm, 24 gm and
26 gm.

you should remember to carry spare stems and flights of your own type, so that you are always prepared should any damage occur to them.

Dartboards

It would be beneficial for you to think seriously about buying a dartboard and fixing it up in your own home. This will have obvious advantages if you are not old enough to go into a public house. Although many youth clubs have a dartboard fixed on the wall somewhere, a lot of young people either: (a) do not belong to such a club, (b) find it very difficult to get on the dartboard for as long as they would like.

Of course, if you are young, you will obviously have to consult your parents about fixing up a board in your home. Perhaps get your father to put it up for you, as it is better to have it exactly the correct distance of throw and height etc.

It may seem overall a very expensive prospect to buy a dartboard, darts, flights, stems and the like, but expenses can be cut. For example, it is possible to start off with perhaps a paper board which is relatively quite cheap and a set of brass darts of which there are many variations. You can graduate from there as you get older, or better, or richer. Of course if you or your parents do not mind the expense of buying a new bristle board and a set of darts then it would be much better, as you will have many hours of enjoyment practising on your board which will take a very long time to wear out. If you take care of your darts they will last you a lifetime.

Top left: Brass barrels, very rarely used in top-class darts nowadays. *Bottom left:* Different patterns of tungsten darts used by many of today's top professionals. *Right:* A wide selection of flights are available.

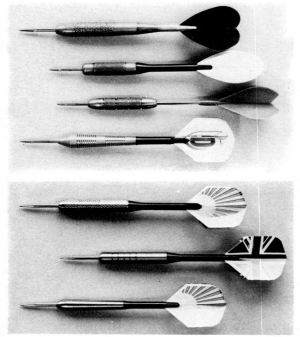

Chapter Seven
Practice

To obtain any success at all in darts or anything else one must participate in a certain amount of practice. When you are starting out it is best to practise as much as possible. However, do not practise for hours on end if you find you are not enjoying it, because this will not help you at all. You will tend just to throw the darts anywhere if you are getting bored, and this sort of practice will do more harm than good.

It is best to get into some kind of rhythm and to try to get on the board every day. The amount of time you practise depends entirely on yourself, but you should try to get in at least an hour a day, if you can.

I have given a timetable of the type of practice that I find best, but you can vary this to suit yourself and your own weaknesses. Apart from the usual kind of practice where you aim at certain numbers for a period of time, play some games of 501 or 1001. See what is the least amount of darts you can finish a game in. This will help you to become more consistent with your play. As you get a little better you will find that you enjoy practising more because at last you are getting some results and if you are the type that likes to keep records you will be able to see your improvement.

Various stances at the oche. *Left:* My own stance, right foot forward, toe pointing almost straight ahead. *Centre left:* A square stance, with both feet up at the oche. *Centre right:* A sideways-on stance, favoured by, among others, Eric Bristow and Tony Brown. *Right:* This stance is not advised. You will find it difficult to make your shots if your 'wrong' foot is ahead of your 'right'.

Throwing action from the front. This is my action, which has no personal frills or idiosyncracies, but which I try to keep as smooth as possible.

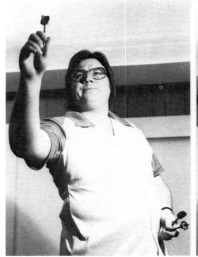

Throwing action from the side. Although it is impossible to lay down rules, as many top players' styles vary, it would be a good idea for a beginner to make a point of standing as still as possible throughout the throw.

Throwing action from the back. I find it important to follow through, and if you study the last two pictures in each sequence you notice that I am following through after delivering the dart.

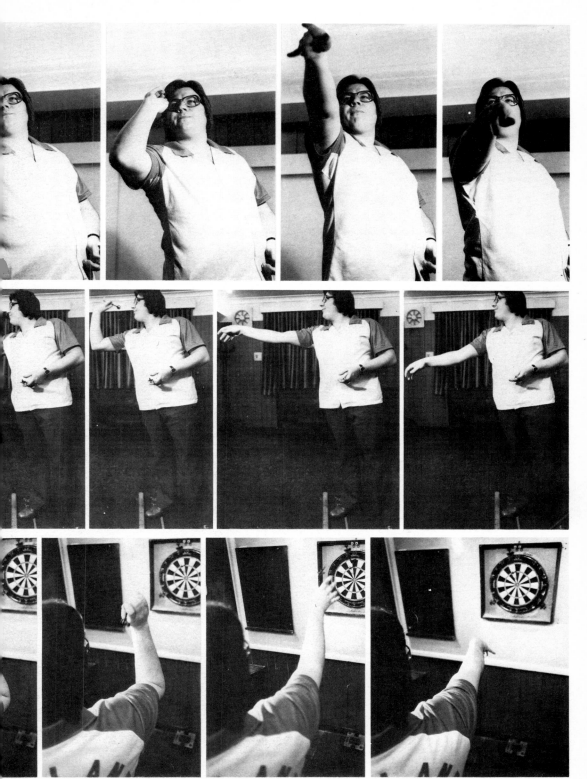

Practice Timetable

1. Ten minutes grouping around the three big trebles, 18, 19 and 20.
2. Ten minutes at 25 and bull.
3. Ten minutes at the most awkward doubles, i.e. 1, 3, 5 etc. These doubles are difficult because if during a game you happen to leave say, 6 and your first dart lands in the single 3, you must then use another dart to even the score.
4. Ten minutes on the most favoured finishing doubles (20, 18, 16).
5. A couple of games of 501 or 1001.
6. A few shots out (i.e. 70 – t10, d20; or 86 – t18, d16).

Read and practise the shots out chart. This will help you to count and to get familiar with the finishing shots, and help with your practice all at the same time.

You must find the grip which seems to favour you. Grips vary among the top players. *Top left:* Eric Bristow has a distinctive grip, with his little finger crooked. *Top right:* My grip is pretty well orthodox, with the barrel gripped about half way down its length. *Bottom left and right:* Some players grip the barrel at the front, others prefer to grip it at the back. John Lowe has special short barrels so that his grip will be the same on each throw.

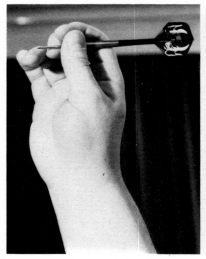

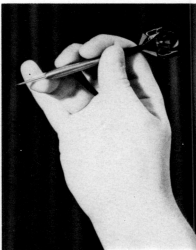

Chapter Eight
Clothing

When playing darts it is obviously best to wear clothes in which you feel comfortable, so that you will be completely at ease and unrestricted. Thus your game will be unaffected by your attire.

Let us first examine what shoes to wear. There could be nothing worse than having a tight-fitting pair of shoes that keep rubbing with each step you take. I personally find a casual soft leather pair the best. You may find training shoes or the like best for you. When you have settled on a pair try to keep them only for when you play darts. This way you get used to them with regard to your

What the well-dressed darter wears. This is actually an England shirt, to which we can all aspire (unless we're Welsh or Scottish or whatever!), but any neat clean short-sleeved shirt will do for the meantime.

'Liberace', or Bobby George, a man who has made his dress his trade-mark. But sequins or no, he is always neat.

own height in relation to the board. If you keep changing, let us suppose, from plimsoles to heeled shoes and back, you will find the relative height of the board varied each time you play.

Now that you have stopped your feet getting corns every time you walk to and from the board, you should get a nice casual shirt to wear. A short sleeve sports shirt is nearly everyone's choice, with perhaps a top pocket for keeping your darts in when not playing. This type of shirt leaves room for movement of the arms. Of course you may prefer to play in long sleeves or a jumper but you will find that some places can get rather warm when you've been playing for a while and a jumper will only make matters worse. Of course, your choice is up to you and what you feel comfortable in.

Now on to trousers. There has been a lot of controversy over recent years regarding jean-type trousers, so much so that the British Darts Organisation have introduced a new ruling which states: 'Dress: jean-type trousers are not permitted during the championship: also we expect all players to be respectfully dressed'. This rule generally applies to the major competitions such as the British Open and World Masters. County players are not permitted to wear jeans and all counties now must have their own strip, as do all International teams. It really does look better with everyone looking the same when attending the games.

Getting back to the question of jeans: if you like wearing them then it will probably be in order to wear them, say, in your local league games. The ruling does apply to women and men alike and I must admit that I agree with it. It would do the image of darts no good at all if Harry Hotdog were to appear on television wearing hobnail boots, a pair of jeans and his lunch plastered down the front of his moth-eaten shirt!

Chapter Nine
Finishing Shots

There have, over the years, been many ideas on different finishing shots. The old fashioned ways of going for shots-out is gradually dying. Many people believed that if a player required say, 67 then the best way to go was treble 19, double 5. Now there is nothing wrong with this providing you can get these shots a reasonable amount of times. My ideas however, are somewhat different because I believe in giving myself as many darts at a double in one throw as possible. If I went for the same 67 and got the treble 19 with my first dart, then in my own estimation I have only one dart left to get the remaining double 5, because there can be no margin of error going for such a double. If you miss and hit a single 5 you then have to even the score up with your last dart. Hence if your opponent is on a double with you, to get another shot you must hope he misses.

So for a shot like 67 I suggest going for treble 17, double 8. Having got the treble 17, you have then got two darts at double 8 and if you miss, you have one dart left to get double 4.

This is only a sample finishing shot. I am merely trying to stress to you that what may seem the most obvious and best way to finish, may not pay the best dividends.

The shots out I have given are standard to all dart players. However, as I stated earlier changes are always occurring and I follow with a few alternatives to use. You may have seen some of the professionals use these finishing shots on television and I myself have had success with them in various tournaments. The finishing shots concerning 91 to 95 are particularly good when you find yourself under pressure from your opponent, i.e. if he is on a double. You will find a 25 or bull easier to hit than a treble. Also should you get it, it almost guarantees you a shot at a double (or bullseye) and obviously it is better to have at least one dart at a double than none at all.

Two of today's stars, who never seem to have much trouble with finishing shots, either calculating them or scoring them, are Jocky Wilson, left, and Nicky Virachkul, right.

Finishing Shots:

170 t20 t20 Bull	117 t20 t17 d8	95 t19 d19	73 t19 d8
167 t20 t19 Bull	117 t20 17 d20	94 18 t20 d8	72 16 16 d20
164 t20 t18 Bull	116 20 t20 d18	94 t18 d20	72 t16 d12
161 t20 t17 Bull	116 t20 16 d20	93 19 t14 d16	71 17 18 d18
160 t20 t20 d20	115 20 t19 d19	93 t19 d18	71 t17 d10
158 t20 t20 d19	115 t20 15 d20	92 20 t16 d12	70 10 20 d20
157 t20 t19 d20	114 20 t18 d20	92 t20 d16	70 t10 d20
156 t20 t20 d18	114 t20 18 d18	91 17 t14 d16	69 19 18 d16
155 t20 t19 d19	113 20 t19 d18	91 t17 d20	69 t19 d6
154 t20 t18 d20	113 t20 13 d20	90 18 t16 d12	69 19 Bull
153 t20 t19 d18	112 20 t20 d16	90 t18 d18	68 20 16 d16
152 t20 t20 d16	112 t20 12 d20	89 19 t10 d20	68 t20 d4
151 t20 t17 d20	111 20 t17 d20	89 t19 d16	67 17 18 d16
150 t20 t18 d18	111 t20 11 d20	89 19 20 Bull	67 t17 d8
149 t20 t19 d16	110 20 t18 d18	88 20 t20 d4	67 17 Bull
148 t20 t20 d14	110 t20 18 d16	88 t20 d14	66 10 16 d20
147 t20 t17 d18	109 20 t19 d16	88 20 18 Bull	66 t10 d18
146 t20 t18 d16	109 t20 17 d16	87 17 t10 d20	65 15 10 d20
145 t20 t15 d20	109 t19 10 d16	87 t17 d18	65 t15 d10
144 t20 t20 d12	108 20 t20 d14	87 17 20 Bull	64 16 16 d16
143 t20 t17 d16	108 t20 16 d16	86 18 t20 d4	64 t16 d8
142 t20 t14 d20	18 t18 d18	86 t18 d16	63 17 6 d20
141 t20 t15 d18	107 20 17 d18	86 18 18 Bull	63 t17 d6
140 t20 t20 d10	107 t20 15 d16	85 15 t10 d20	62 10 12 d20
139 t20 t13 d20	107 t19 18 d16	85 t15 d20	62 t10 d16
138 t20 t18 d12	106 20 t18 d16	85 15 20 Bull	61 15 6 d20
137 t20 t15 d16	106 t20 6 d20	84 t20 d12	61 t15 d8
136 t20 t20 d8	105 20 t15 d20	84 20 14 Bull	60 20 d20
135 t20 t17 d12	105 t20 13 d16	83 t17 d16	59 19 d20
134 t20 t14 d16	104 20 t20 d12	83 17 16 Bull	58 18 d20
133 t20 t19 d8	104 t18 18 d16	82 t14 d20	57 17 d20
132 t20 t16 d12	103 20 t17 d16	82 14 18 Bull	56 16 d20
131 t20 t17 d10	103 t20 3 d20	81 t15 d18	55 15 d20
130 t20 t18 d8	102 20 t14 d20	81 15 16 Bull	54 18 d18
129 t19 t16 d12	102 t20 10 d16	80 t20 d10	53 13 d20
128 t18 t14 d16	101 20 t15 d18	80 20 20 d20	52 12 d20
127 t20 t17 d8	101 t20 1 d20	80 t16 d16	51 11 d20
126 t20 t10 d18	101 t17 18 d16	79 19 20 d20	50 18 d16
125 t20 t15 d10	100 20 t20 d10	79 t19 d11	49 17 d16
124 t20 t16 d8	100 20 t16 d16	78 18 20 d20	48 16 d16
123 t19 t10 d18	100 t20 d20	78 t18 d12	47 15 d16
122 t20 t10 d16	99 19 t16 d16	77 19 18 d20	46 6 d20
121 t20 t15 d8	99 t19 10 d16	77 t19 d10	45 13 d16
120 t20 20 d20	98 20 t18 d12	76 20 16 d20	44 12 d16
119 19 t20 d20	98 t20 d19	76 t20 d8	43 3 d20
119 t19 t10 d16	97 19 t18 d12	75 17 18 d20	42 10 d16
119 t19 12 Bull	97 t19 d20	75 t17 d12	41 9 d16
118 18 t20 d20	96 20 t20 d8	74 14 20 d20	40 d20
118 t18 14 Bull	96 t20 d18	74 t14 d16	
117 20 t19 d20	95 19 t20 d8	73 19 18 d18	

Variations on Finishing Shots:

135 25 t20 Bull	126 Bull t20 d8	95 25 20 Bull	93 Bull 3 d20
135 Bull t15 d20	125 25 t20 d20	95 Bull 13 d16	92 25 17 Bull
132 25 t19 Bull	125 Bull t17 d12	94 25 19 Bull	92 Bull 10 d16
132 Bull t14 d20	125 Bull 25 Bull	94 Bull 12 d16	91 25 16 Bull
132 Bull Bull d16	122 18 t18 Bull	93 25 18 Bull	91 Bull 9 d16
126 19 t19 Bull	121 t20 11 Bull		

Chapter Ten
Common Courtesy

Every sport has its unwritten laws concerning common courtesy, and darts is no different. There are quite a few people around who will try to distract their opponents in the hope of winning the game but they only succeed in getting a bad reputation and also they are only fooling themselves into believing that they are better than they really are. No matter how good or bad a player you may be there is no reason whatever to try to win any type of game, whether friendly or competitive, by using foul means.

I have given a few particulars here of the type of things you should bear in mind. Treat your opponents and other players as you would want to be treated yourself.

1 If you smoke, it is very bad to blow smoke either in the direction of your opponent or at the dartboard, when you have finished taking your throw and are retrieving your darts. This can be very unpleasant for someone who does not smoke. If you are smoking a cigar, where the smoke tends to linger, it can be very off-putting and can impair the vision of your opponent.

2 After retrieving your darts it is better to walk up the side of the throwing area and not directly in front of your opponent as he may

Spectators have an obligation to be courteous, particularly by refraining to make a noise during play.

Chalking the barrels for better grip is a good idea if your hands are inclined to sweat. Soaking the chalk will prevent dust sticking to the board.

be a quick thrower and be waiting on the oche ready to take his shot. By walking directly in front of him, he will obviously have to move and this may spoil his rhythm in the game.

3 Always stand behind the person who is throwing and not alongside or in front of the oche. It can be very distracting if a player can see his opponent out of the corner of his eye when on the oche waiting to take his shot. There should be only two people between the oche and the dartboard and they are the scorer and the caller.

4 While your opponent is taking his shot, never rattle loose change in your pockets, deliberately fiddle with your darts, chink glasses or make any unnecessary sounds which might disturb him.

5 Unless it is a friendly match where practically anything goes, and really is exactly what it means: 'a friendly', never talk to your opponent. It may not affect you and may even alleviate your nerves, but it may be extremely off-putting to your opponent. I do not want you to get the wrong idea here: you do not have to be a complete robot while playing, but it is better to be courteous and not be a nuisance. After all, your opponent wants to win as much as you do and surely there can be no pleasure in winning a game by foul means.

6 If you are a player who uses chalk on darts, you will know or soon notice that some of the chalk invariably comes off the barrels and sticks to the dartboard as your darts hit the board. There are different ways to combat this, for instance: (a) Soak a stick of chalk for a couple of minutes in water. After applying the chalk to the barrels, the feel of the chalk will be no different and may even prove better for you. The chalk will, however, stick to the barrels and no dust will come off when a dart hits the board; (b) Like many players now, use candle wax instead of chalk on your barrels. Slippery wax does help the grip of the dart and you will find it gives a very nice feel to the barrels. It is very simple to melt a candle into any kind of mould, i.e. an old tablespoon etc., which will quite easily fit into your pocket and be available for use as required.

7 If you are a spectator, you may be cheering on one of the players or perhaps one of the teams. There is obviously nothing wrong in this whatsoever and indeed adds to the excitement as the game proceeds. However, it is not good practice to call out while a player is in the process of a throw. Wait until the player has completed his throw before calling out. The same goes if you notice an error on the scoreboard. Wait until the player has taken his shot before bringing it to the attention of the scorer.

8 If you are yourself scoring or calling a game try to keep as still as possible. I know this sounds hard, but gradually as you get into the game it will seem much easier.

These are as I have said a few unwritten rules because they seem obvious to most players and spectators alike, but it must be said that these rules do get broken from time to time, whether intentionally or not.

Chapter Eleven
Fitness

Although you may have seen, read or heard about professional darts players keeping fit, I can assure you that this consideration is not really part of their make-up. I am not saying that they do not *try* to keep fit, but it is extremely hard to find the time to take any great deal of exercise, i.e. walking, jogging or just plain 'physical jerks' during the day. The reason for this is that being a professional player means that you always have a great deal to do in the way of travelling around for exhibitions and tournaments.

Naturally, in any spare time, if you really have any as a professional, you could indulge in a swim at your local baths or even go for a long walk, but of course unless this is regular exercise it will be a sheer waste of time.

If you are an ordinary darts player who goes to work every day and plays darts in the evening, you too will find it very hard to find the time to exercise, unless you play only one or two nights per week, leaving free other evenings for any form of exercise you might fancy. If you are a serious player it is better to take in exercises which do not affect your arms to the extent of making them weary, so as to impair your throwing action. Sports such as badminton, tennis and squash, unless you played them before you took up darts, will probably be harmful to your game. The reason for this is that you will use muscles that you did not realise existed and your throwing action will suffer if you ache.

Unless you are totally out of condition, your fitness will probably not affect your game. Even in long one day open events you are not playing darts all day, and if you are fortunate enough to win through to the final you will find, on looking back, that you have not really played a great deal of games.

There is one thing you must remember and that is that whatever exercise you care to take, it is best not to overdo it. Health-wise it is obviously beneficial to be your 'correct' weight as far as you can. If you are greatly overweight try to lose a few pounds or stones, whichever suits your description. Otherwise in the long events you may find yourself a little tired. This is not due to the games you have played, it is due to standing around on your feet for most of the day. However, if you are naturally a big person, like many of our leading players, you may care to stay that way. I have personally found myself tiring in the latter stages of tournaments and so at the time of writing I am on a diet, hoping to lose two stone. Darts is a wonderful sport which has progressed extraordinarily over recent years, and it is far better, and I am sure you will agree, to live your life to the full and try to be fairly active, so as to enjoy darts for the rest of your days.

Chapter Twelve
Games to Play

Here are a few simple games that can be played on the dartboard. They can be played for their own sake, or to add interest to practice sessions. Try them at your local or even at home.

Fox and Hounds

Two players 'bull up' (i.e. throw for the bull) and the nearest player to the bull represents the fox, whilst the further is the hound. The fox commences on double 20 and travels in an anticlockwise direction. He must get each double and a single in turn, the object being to get back to the 20 mark. The hound commences on 18 (being two numbers behind the 20) and chases the fox also in an anti-clockwise direction. The hound has to get only the double of each number, and must try to catch the fox as quickly as possible. When the hound catches the fox the roles are reversed. The winner is the player (acting as the fox) who gets the furthest.

Grand National

This game can be played with any number of players. The object is to jump the fences and complete the course first. Only the inner part of the singles segments and the trebles 13, 17, 8 and 5 are used. The course is: small 20, 1, 18, 4, treble 13 (first fence), small 6, 10, 15, 2, treble 17 (second fence), small 3, 19, 7, 16, treble 8 (third fence), small 11, 14, 9, 12, treble 5 (fourth fence) and finish on a bull. Should a player miss the required number in three throws (nine darts) then his horse has fallen and he is out of the race. This does not include the bull finish.

Snooker

The board is set up with the numbers 1 to 15 which represent the reds on a snooker table and each count as 1. The numbers 16 to 25 represent the colours and score as follows: 16 yellow (scores 2); 17 green (3); 18 brown (4); 19 blue (5); 20 pink (6); 25 black (7). The first player has to pot any red (any number between 1 and 15) by scoring three darts in the segment either with three singles, a double and a single or a treble. He can then go for any colour of his choice which he must nominate and scores in the same way. As in snooker the reds 'stay down' when potted and when they have all gone the colours are potted in order of value, yellow to black. Should a player throwing for a red, miss with all three darts, then this counts as 4 away to his opponent. The bull scores as 2×25.

Killer

This game is played on doubles only. To start the game each player has to throw a dart with his 'wrong' hand. Wherever the dart lands becomes 'his' double. Each player then has to try for his own particular double. Once he has obtained this he becomes a 'killer', and then aims for the doubles of the other players. Players have five 'lives' and each time a 'killer' hits their double they lose a life. The winner is the one who still has 'lives' when everyone else has none.

Round the Board

Each player simply works his way around the board from 1 to 20, finishing with a 25 and bull. It is a race, and the first player to hit the bull wins. This game can also be played on trebles or doubles to make it a little harder.

Noughts and Crosses

This is another simple game for either two players or two teams. It is played in exactly the same way as the ordinary noughts and crosses and the winner is the person, or team, to be the first to complete a line, either across, down or diagonally. Instead of a noughts and a crosses box, different segments of the board are used. Here is an example of how the scoreboard is set up:

d20	t13	d10
d7	Bull	d18
t3	d2	t14

When a player hits the required number then a nought or cross, or even the player's initials, is put in its place until a line is completed. Any combinations of numbers can be substituted for the example given above.

Beat the Score

Each player is given five 'lives' and the object is to beat the score of the previous player. Failure to do so means the loss of a life. If a player scores 100 or over and the next in his turn equals that score, a life is not taken away. The last player with a life left wins.

Battlefield

The object of this game is to defeat your opponent's army. One player has the top half of the board (11 round to 13) and the other has the lower half (6 round to 8). Each player has ten soldiers which are represented by numbers in his half. The player chooses ten areas (singles, doubles or trebles) in his half of the board and writes them next to his name on the marking board. Players then throw alternately in an attempt to kill off the opponent's army.

Halve it

This game has grown more popular in the last few years due to the fact that it is one of the games played in the British Pentathlon, an annual competition which is run by the Kent Darts Organisation to find the best all round player. There are of course different variations on the game but I have illustrated it as it would be played in the Pentathlon.

Each player throws alternately, aiming to score as many of the designated target as possible. For example, his first three darts will be thrown at single 20, and if two are successful, he will have 40 entered on the scoreboard. Each player scores for each of the seven rounds. Should a player miss the required number on any round then his score on all previous rounds is halved.

Stars from Wales and Scotland. Ceri Morgan (top), of the unorthodox throw, and Scotland's Rab Smith (below).

	Player A	Player B
20		
16		
d 7		
14		
t10		
17		
Bull		

35

Chapter Thirteen

Tournaments

There are throughout the year many, many tournaments which anyone can enter. These 'opens' are usually run by the officials of the county in which the tournament is held and the name of the competition usually goes under the county's name, e.g. The Kent Open. There are of course other tournaments at home and abroad which carry very good prize money. These are run by independent people, and if they are run smoothly and gain a good reputation then usually the competitions are held annually.

However there are the better tournaments which are usually sponsored and these boast prize money which goes into *thousands*. Most of these are televised and thus the B.D.O. reserve the right to seed players, as is the practice in tennis, to give the better players a better chance of reaching the final stages. Probably the tournaments carrying the most prestige are the Embassy World Professional and the Winmau World Masters. Here I give a brief description of these tournaments together with a few more.

World Professional

The Embassy World Professional Tournament is exactly what it says. This competition brings together the world's best professionals to compete on a knock-out basis till the winner alone is left. The first one was held in 1978, when a big, happy-go-lucky chap from Wales became Champion of the World. His name is Leighton Rees and he dazzled the audiences on British television with a brilliant display of throwing which lasted all week (the duration of the championship). Even in the final he produced brilliant darts to destroy an on-form John Lowe. This tournament was very important to Leighton, not only for the money that came

A scene from the *News of the World* championship of 1977 held at the Alexandra Palace, London. This is one of the oldest and most respected championships.

Eric Bristow and Bobby George being introduced to the crowd at the 1980 Embassy World Professional Tournament final.

from winning. To be champion of all the professionals is one of the greatest achievements of any player's life. The B.D.O. run this tournament, and having taken part in it myself I can say that they are as professional in their own right as the players taking part.

World Masters

Entry into this competition is by a knock-out system which begins first in one's own county. The winners go through to the county play-offs. Players who win major titles such as the British Open, World Professional or Marlboro Masters etc., are seeded through to the World play-offs. Players play the best of three legs, best of three sets, 501 up. Invitations are given to players who are in the world rankings as well as to many overseas champions. The first winner of this championship was Devon's Cliff Inglis. At that time the championship was known as the Phonogram World Masters. In 1976 Winmau stepped in to sponsor the championship.

British Pentathlon

The first British Pentathlon took place in 1976 at the Star Hotel, Maidstone, Kent. Twenty top players were chosen from an original list of those who had expressed their wish to enter. The heading of 'put up or shut up' appeared in the national newspapers regarding the pentathlon because of its entry fee of £100. The actual competition is a series of games of 501, 1001, 2001, Shanghai, Halve-it, and Round the Board on Doubles. Every player plays each other and points are awarded for the quickest legs, scores of 100, 140, and 180 etc. The outright winner at the end of a very long day's play is the one with the most points. Prizes are given to the first four, with individual prizes for the best Shanghai, Round the Board on Doubles and Halve-it games.

British Open

This competition, which is usually held at the beginning of every new year, is open to *all* players everywhere. There is a men's singles, men's pairs, ladies' singles, ladies' pairs and a mixed triple event. It is held in London over a period of two or three days. The prize money is very good for all finalists, and the winners of the men's events are seeded through to the World Masters.

Chapter Fourteen
Rules

When entering any B.D.O. event, there are rules that apply to all players regarding equipment, clothing and general rules relating to the competition. It would be a long and tedious task to print all the rules to every tournament here and you would be thoroughly bored with reading them! So, I have listed just a few which are the most important and beneficial for you to know.

The British Darts Organisation Rules apply as at August, 1980
B.D.O. Playing Rules
All darts events in Great Britain under the exclusive supervision of the British Darts Organisation Limited shall be run under the following playing rules.
General Playing Rules
(a) Players shall provide their own darts, which shall not exceed an overall maximum length of 30·5 cm (12 in) not weigh more than 50 grammes. Each dart shall consist of a needle-type point, which shall be rigidly fixed to a barrel. At the rear of the barrel, shall be an attached flighted stem, which may consist of up to two separate pieces (i.e. a flight and a stem).
(b) Players shall have the right to request a check on the height of dartboard, and the distance from the throwing line (oche).
(c) The British Darts Organisation Limited reserves the right to seed players, or teams, in certain events when deemed necessary.
(d) All players, or teams, shall play within the playing rules, and where necessary any supplementary rules laid down in an entry form, or programme.
(e) All trophies awarded to a player, or team, are to be retained, unless they are of a challenge, or perpetual type, when such trophies are to be returned to the organisers on request.
(f) Any player, or team, failing to comply with any of the B.D.O. playing rules during an event shall be liable to disqualification from that event.
(g) The interpretation of the B.D.O. playing rules in relation to a darts event shall be determined by the darts event organisers, whose decision shall be final and binding.
(h) Any matter not expressly covered by the B.D.O. playing rules shall be determined by the B.D.O. board of directors, whose decision on all such matters shall be final and binding.
(i) The term 'organisers' shall mean the British Darts Organisation Limited, its officials, or persons appointed by the British Darts Organisation Limited to carry out its functions in relation to darts events.

Throw: (a) All darts must be thrown by, and from, the player's hand.

(b) A throw shall consist of three darts, unless a leg, set, or match, is finished in less than three darts.

(c) Any dart bouncing off, or falling out of the dartboard, does not count, and shall not be rethrown.

Tournament and Championship Playing Rules (General)

Entry: (a) Admission fees to tournament venues are not refundable.

(b) All entries must be made on an official B.D.O. entry form, fully completed, which must be returned, together with the appropriate entry fee, before or on the specified closing date.

(c) No entry will be accepted unless strictly in accordance with the requirements laid down on the entry form.

(d) Only the players named on an entry form as the competing individual or team, shall be eligible to play in the respective darts event.

(e) No player, or team, shall enter more than once in any respective darts event.

(f) No player shall play in more than one team in any respective darts event.

(g) All players participating in an individual darts event must play under their own name.

Registration: (a) All tournament players, or teams, shall register at each darts event at the scheduled times predetermined by the B.D.O.-appointed organisers.

(b) Any tournament player, ot team, failing to register by the notified time shall be eliminated from that tournament, in which event no entry fees shall be refundable.

(c) Only THREE minutes shall be allowed from the time of calling over the public address system for the player, or team, to reach the control desk, or assigned match board, whichever requirement is being called for.

(d) The B.D.O.-appointed organisers reserve the right to alter the scheduled times and playing format whenever it is deemed necessary.

(e) Any player, or team, has the right to be advised the time of the next game that the player, or team, is scheduled to play.

Draw: (a) There will be only one draw for opponents which shall be conducted prior to the darts event – the bracket system being adopted.

(b) Draw sheets must be displayed, where possible, at the control desk, in the event programme, at the match board or at a convenient point in the venue.

(c) No substitutes shall be allowed in an individual darts event.

(d) No substitutes shall be allowed after the first round of a team event, unless the playing rules of the particular event allow reserve members of a team to be used, or in extenuating circumstances, allowed at the discretion of the B.D.O.-appointed organisers.

Order of Play: (a) The order of play shall be determined by a draw, or by the toss of a coin, at the control desk, prior to the issue of a match assignment card.

(b) The winner of the draw, or toss, shall throw first in the first leg/set and all odd alternate legs/sets thereafter in the first match.

(c) The loser of the draw, or toss, shall throw first in the second leg/set and if applicable in alternate even legs/sets, thereafter in that respective match.

Practice: (a) Each player, or team, is entitled to six practice darts to be thrown at the assigned match board prior to the match commencing.

(b) No practice shall be allowed on the unassigned match boards after the darts event has officially started.

(c) Practice boards shall be provided in or adjacent to the tournament room for the exclusive use of tournament players, or teams.

Tournament Play: (a) In tournament play all players, or teams, shall play under the supervision and direction of B.D.O.-appointed organisers and officials.

(b) A player's opponent must stand at least 610 mm (2 ft) to the rear of the thrower at the oche.

(c) In 'stage finals' the players, or teams, shall conduct their play under the supervision and direction of stage officials, and in between throws shall be located in such a position as to afford an unrestricted view of the proceedings for players, officials, spectators, and, in some darts events, for television cameras.

(d) No prompting shall be allowed from any person.

(e) A player at the oche is entitled to consult with the referee, or caller, on the amount scored, or required, at any time during the throw. However the player shall not be advised on how to check out.

(f) A player attaining a score of 180 shall be eligible to receive a 'BDO 180' cloth badge by presenting a match result/score sheet, duly asigned by a B.D.O.-appointed organiser, to the control desk. (This is applicable to B.D.O.-appointed darts events only.)

Playing Attire: (a) The wearing of jeans, or denim-type trousers is not permitted.

(b) No headgear shall be worn, without the prior permission of the B.D.O.-appointed organisers (a member of the Sikh religion would qualify for such permission).

(c) All players, or teams, representing their county at regional play-offs and grand finals shall wear their county-approved playing attire.

(d) All players, or teams, representing their country in a B.D.O. darts event shall wear their country-approved playing attire.

(e) County, and country organisers are recommended to have 'unmarked' playing attire available for those occasions when advertising rights are likely to be infringed.

Advertising: (a) The B.D.O.-appointed organisers reserve the

One of the officials made familiar in Britain by television: referee Tony Green.

right to protect the sponsor's interest with regard to any advertising material used during a B.D.O. darts event by the players, teams, organisers, or their sponsors during a B.D.O. darts event.

(b) Players and spectators will not be allowed to wear any clothing that advertises a marketable product or concern, without the prior permission of the B.D.O.-appointed organisers.

(c) The B.D.O.-appointed organisers reserve the right to all advertising in connection with any B.D.O. darts event.

(d) Players that qualify for a televised 'stage final' will not be allowed to wear any advertising, or apparel which advertises, any marketable product, or concern.

Amendments/Additions: (a) The British Darts Organisation Limited reserves the right to add to, or amend, any, or all, of the B.D.O. playing rules at any time to meet any purposes deemed to be necessary at that time.

Copyright: (a) The entire contents of the B.D.O. playing rules are the copyright of the British Darts Organisation Limited and may not be reprinted, copied, duplicated, or otherwise reproduced wholly, or in part, without the written consent of the copyright owner.

(b) When a darts event is being staged outside of the jurisdiction of the B.D.O. the organisers of that darts event may be given consent to state that 'B'D'O' playing rules apply' on entry forms, and other event literature. Consent to do this can only be obtained by making an application in writing to the B.D.O. Headquarters.

As I have already stated these rules are by no means complete, but the ones I have included will keep you in good stead for any major or minor turnament. A complete copy of the Rules can be found in the B.D.O. Official Darts Diary which can be obtained from the B.D.O. Headquarters, 2 Pages Lane, Muswell Hill, London N10 1PS, England. Telephone: 01-883 5544.

Chapter Fifteen
The British Darts Organisation

The British Darts Organisation was formed in 1973 to administer inter-county leagues and other national competitions. Ten areas were originally interested: London, Kent, Surrey, Herts, Cheshire, West Midlands, West of England, S.W. Lancs, Wales and Devon. Later, however, due to team difficulties, Wales were forced to drop out and Thames Valley took their place. The first objective of the B.D.O. was the inter-counties competition which commenced on 7 October 1973 with a season of nine matches. The teams consisted of twelve players who played the best of 3 legs 501. To begin with, 'B' teams were not included: it was thought 'B' matches could possibly take place through individual challenges. The same theory applied to the ladies, but as most of the ten teams who set up the B.D.O. had ladies interested in playing it was decided that a separate championship be commenced for them. They played the ladies' games during the intervals of the inter-county matches. The ladies' team consisted of four players, who played 801 up best of 3 legs.

Players were asked to sign an optional 'contract' to allow the B.D.O. to act for them. Commercial interests were entering into competition darts, and the B.D.O. could therefore safeguard the players' interests.

The inter-county league got off to a good start, having only one setback when the West Midlands team dropped out at the last moment. However, Somerset put in a team and the ten teams who took part in the very first inter-county matches were: Lancashire, Surrey, West of England, Devon, London, Kent, Cheshire, Thames Valley, Hertfordshire and Somerset.

That first year both the men's and ladies' championships went to the North of England, Lancashire winning the men's section and Cheshire the ladies' section.

The next season saw the number of championship contenders double to 20 teams. The original ten continued to play each other and the new counties played each other in a new section. At the end of the season the leaders of the two sections played off for the B.D.O. Championship. The ladies' championship continued but after several complaints the format was changed to four single games of 1 leg 501.

The 1975/76 season saw a big change come about in the inter-county league. With a total now of 31 teams the league was divided into four groups, Red, White, Blue and Gold and again a play-off took place at the end of the season between the winners of each.

Over the next few years various changes were made. At the present time the league boasts a total of 47 county teams and is made up of five different groups: a Premier Division (which contains the ten strongest county teams) Division 1 (South), Division 2 (South), Division 1 (North) and Division 2 (North). Each county now has an 'A' and 'B' team for both men and women.

In 1979 the Premier League men's 'A' teams began to play the best of 5 legs 501 as it was felt this would produce more competitive darts. The ladies' teams which used to have four players went up to five players who play the best of 3 legs 501.

The inter-county league thrives and it must be every Super League player's ambition to play county darts because it is from the county teams that the international players are chosen.

In 1973 the first home international took place in Bristol and was organised by the West of England Darts Organisation. The teams consisted of seven players who each played one game of 801 and the throw was 7 ft 6 in. It was hoped at this time that the championship would become a regular yearly occurrence. The England team, which contained players like Tommy O'Regan and Cliff Inglis, took the title. The Championship became a yearly event and in 1974 was held in London at the Lyceum Ballroom. This turned out to be a real cliff hanger but England managed to retain the title.

In 1975 Wales won the Championship on their home ground of Cardiff to the great delight of 2,000 fans.

A popular Australian player, Terry O'Dea has played darts round the world and is well known in Britain where he appears in the major televised championships.

Stefan Lord, from Sweden, is a former *News of the World* winner who plays regularly on the international circuit.

In 1976 the format was changed to the best of 3 legs 501 and this time England and Scotland shared the title in Dundee.

Wales once again took the title in 1977 and again it was in front of a home crowd, this time at Swansea.

In 1978, England, having won all three matches, took the title with a clear lead of 6 points over Wales. This Championship was held in Morecambe and once again the format was changed to the best of 3 legs 601.

England retained the title in 1979 in Edinburgh in front of a very disappointing crowd of only 1,400.

1980 saw Northern Ireland entering their team for the Championship in Cork. This now makes a total of five national teams in one of the most popular annual events.

World Darts Federation

This body was formed in 1976 and had the unanimous support of 15 countries. It was intended to bring a bit of dignity to the game. It was felt darts could no longer be regarded as merely a pub game. It was a sport that it was hoped might be included in the Olympics in the not too distant future.

The president elected was Shan David of South Africa, and Olly Croft was voted as general secretary. The 15 countries represented were: Australia, Belgium, Bermuda, Gibraltar, Denmark, England, Canada, Ireland, Scotland, Malta, New Zealand, South Africa, Sweden, U.S.A. and Wales.

There was a lot of discussion at this time about the different throws adopted. In the Home Counties Championships the 7 ft 6 in throw was used, whereas overseas 8 ft was almost universal. So in 1978 the World Darts Federation decided that a compromise had to be made and therefore a throw of 7 ft $9\frac{1}{4}$ in or 2·37 metres was introduced and it is now used throughout Great Britain by the British Darts Organisation.

The first international match against the U.S.A. took place on 15 March 1974 at the Royal Manhattan Hotel in New York. Although Great Britain had a strong team they lost 8–6 to the Americans.

International matches are now held throughout the year on a regular basis between England, Scotland, Ireland and Wales and the B.D.O./A.D.O. stage a competition between players from Great Britain and America when the B.D.O. tour is on during August of each year.

World Cup

This tournament was first held in December 1977 and Wales turned out to be the eventual winners. Held at the Wembley Conference Centre, it consisted of a team, pairs and singles events on a knock-out basis. The World Darts Federation then decided that this competition should be staged every two years and hence in 1979 it took place in the plush Space Centre at the Sahara Hotel in Las Vegas. England took the title quite comfortably with a lead of 46 points over their nearest rivals, America.

Chapter Sixteen
The Unknowns

You might not have heard of many of the players in this chapter, but I can assure you that they are not only top class county players but could quite easily be selected to play for their country at any time now or in the future, and would put up a good all round performance.

There are many players who, although they have the ability, unfortunately never get selected to play for their country simply because: (a) everyone who plays well could not possibly play for say, England, otherwise the team would consist of about 100 or so players; (b) selection rests solely on the ability to play well consistently at inter-county matches throughout a season, hence only county players are put forward for the selectors to choose from.

The players discussed here are a few of the better players I have had the pleasure of playing against on my travels. At the time of compiling this book, none of them has yet represented his country, but I feel sure it is only a matter of time for some.

The Yorkshire county team is one of the strongest and I have selected three who I have seen in action many times.

Brian Langworth (Yorkshire)
Brian is one of the best money players around and is always about when there is a challenge on. He is something of a legend around South Yorkshire and folk in that part of the country regard him quite simply as 'world class'.

Brian Langworth lost a chance of winning the 1979 British Open by not going for a bull. He set up his double, but Tony Brown stepped in to win.

Brian has a fairly unusual way of sticking his darts in the board. They hang down whereas most players' darts either enter the board straight or stick up slightly. This by no means affects his ability to hit many maximum scores and his method has proved to be very successful for him and over the years made him a very competitive player. Brian has been around quite some time in the dart world and has won many, many trophies. Some of his best achievements are Yorkshire Individual Champion in 1976, 1977 and 1978; Derbyshire Individual Champion in 1976 and 1977; he won the Milton Keynes open pairs with his friend Alan Smith in 1979. Probably Brian's biggest success to date was being runner-up to Tony Brown in the 1979 British Open. He was particularly unfortunate to lose as towards the end of the game he 'played safe' and left himself a double when he really should have gone for a bullseye with his last dart. Hence Tony Brown finished the match and became the British Open Champion with his next throw. Undoubtedly this was a mistake that Brian will never forget or make again.

Tony Littlewood (Yorkshire)

Tony is another good money player and is also a very good competition player. I myself know full well Tony's ability as I played him in the final of the Leicestershire Open in 1979 and although I scored consistently well it was simply not good enough and I lost 3–0 without even getting a shot at a double! I have since played Tony in a county match when Kent played Yorkshire and got my own back by beating him 3–0, emphasising the charm of the game of darts: one minute you are winning, the next minute you are losing.

Tony is a great friend of Brian Langworth and they have often played in pairs together. He is a very serious player and rarely seems to smile, which I put down to total concentration throughout a tournament. Tony has been travelling around picking up many open competition titles and he is quite capable of turning on the 'magic' in the very last stages of a tournament after playing consistently well all day. He is a very tough competitor and I am sure he will get his England place before his career is over.

Tony Bowers (Yorkshire)

I first met Tony at Pontins Holiday Village, Prestatyn, when we were part of a four-man team with Paul Reynolds of Yorkshire and Tony Clark of Wales.

My first impression of Tony, watching him practise, was that we had picked a right loser, and I told him this a long time afterwards, when I got to know him a bit better! The reason for my assumption was his style: he has one of the most unusual ways of throwing a dart that I have ever seen. He seems to jog about on the oche from left to right before he throws. In fact in Yorkshire his nickname is 'Rocker'. I was convinced that when Tony stepped up to take his throw the scorer was about to get a dart in his right ear! However, Tony's first shot produced 180 and when it came to

his turn again he scored the winning double. Unfortunately in the next round we were to lose and I did not see Tony play again until I met him at Ladbrokes Holiday Village in Norfolk. Tony reached the finals, although he could hardly speak because of the cold he had. However, when he stepped up to the oche in the final he produced some magnificent throwing and took the singles title very convincingly indeed.

Tony has progressed by leaps and bounds since he was 18 years old playing on a double board. He was part of the Yorkshire team which won the N.D.A.G.B. six-man team event and has also been runner up in the Nodor 4s. He won the National Kwiz pairs title with John Hawkins in 1979; has qualified three times for Yorkshire in the Marlboro Masters, won the Merseyside Open in 1979, was Yorkshire's representative in the Embassy L.V. 1979 and was Yorkshire *News of the World* Champion 1980. Although his style is somewhat unusual and unbalanced, he is a very competent and outstanding player indeed.

Joe Dodd (Oxfordshire)

Joe is a big lad of about 6 ft 3 in and 20 stone, who plays consistently well for Oxfordshire in the British Darts Organisation inter-county league, and indeed, at one stage had only lost one game in four years! I have only played Joe twice. The first time was in an open competition held on the Isle of Sheppey in Kent, and the second was in the final of the London and Home Counties Divisional finals of the 1980 *News of the World* at Battersea Town Hall, London. Both times, luckily, I happened to be in top form and won. However, I can say here and now that he is one of the toughest players I have ever played against. Take for instance the London and Home Counties final. Joe, having won the toss, took the first leg in 16 darts. I won the second in 14 darts and the third in 17 darts and Joe was on a double in both legs! He is a very quiet person who never has a bad word for anybody. At his best he

Left: A familiar experience for Tony Littlewood — being congratulated by the sponsor after another win. *Right:* Tony Bowers is also no stranger to victory — here he is with the handsome *News of the World* Yorkshire championship cup in 1980.

can produce many maximum scores and really only needs a break in one big tournament to establish himself in the top class. This came closer in 1981 when he was picked to join the England squad.

Denis Ovens (London)

If there were an award for changing attitude and appearance overnight then it would certainly go to Denis! I am not committing libel by writing in this manner about Denis as what I am about to state is totally agreeable to him. Up to 1980, Denis used to play in competitions in old jeans, boots and with hair and a beard like 'Catweazle', and he was also one of the most disagreeable people you could ever wish to encounter. Tell Denis 'It's a nice day' and he would reply: 'I thought it was rather lousy myself' – but this was the 'old' Denis.

As if by some miracle he has changed his appearance and attitude towards the game. He is now a very talkative and agreeable person whose appearance is first class. His ability has also changed. From being a good pub player and average county player he is now a very competent tournament player who is knocking on the door for an England shirt. He is definitely one to be wary of in open competitions as his consistency over a long period of time is quite exceptional. I know Denis very well and have had the pleasure of partnering him in a couple of tournaments which, I am glad to say, we won. He does not bother in the least about who he has to play against and fears nobody. He is also a good money player and for this sort of game you must have nerves of steel.

From being a very brash youngster he seems to have matured overnight and now has an edge to his dart playing skill. He will only get better as time goes by, and we could see Denis in the top ten of the world in the not too distant future.

John Avery (Hampshire)

John is one of the better county players that I have seen and I think him rather unlucky not to have been selected to play for his country yet. In all the games he has played for Sussex I think you can count on one hand the games he has lost. He is quite an exceptional player who travels all over the country and abroad to compete in tournaments.

He is a land surveyor by trade and once emigrated to Australia for a period of four years where he actually played professional football for Yugal-Prague. He is a bit of an all-round sportsman and once represented Sussex schoolboys in long distance running. He lives in Chichester, Sussex and although he has had a very good run for Sussex County has decided to commit himself now to Hampshire. In two seasons for Sussex he lost only one game, to yours truly, in inter-county matches, and has been voted Man of the Match no less than eleven times. He was Sussex player of the year in 1978 and represented the B.D.O. touring party in 1980, winning all three of his matches against the U.S.A. team.

His ambition, quite simply, is to play for England and after

being very successful in his county matches and open competitions I am sure we will see him wearing an England strip in the not too distant future.

Ron Cavill

Ron is without a shadow of a doubt the worst competition player in the world but his total dedication makes him worthy of a mention. Ron, as it happens, is my future father-in-law and is a great sport and would certainly not mind my writing about him in this manner. The reason I am in fact writing this is because not everybody can become a champion, and yet everybody has the opportunity of entering competitions and enjoying themselves. It is players like Ron who make up the numbers, and without bad players and the lesser-known players, profesionals could not survive.

'One Round Ron' as he is better known, is a funny little man who plays darts regularly in his local league. He is very rarely seen off the board at the Ponders End Smallholders Club which is Ron's local in Enfield. He loves the game, and with a laugh and a grin will tell you how bad a player he is. He has now reached the stage where he is frightened of winning a game just in case he loses his nickname!

Ron is an example of the many players who love to watch, read about and take part in our sport and who know deep down that they will never progress from being mediocre. I thank players like Ron and respect them as much as I respect the top players, because their hearts and souls are in the game as much as those of John Lowe or Eric Bristow or anyone else who plays.

Left: Joe Dodd, who, with his partner Sue Morgan, finished runners-up in the Marlboro mixed pairs championship of 1980.

Right: An all-round sportsman, John Avery has found his greatest skill lies in throwing darts.

Left: Ron Cavill, undoubtedly one of the worst of current competing darts players.

Right: Lew Walker, in my opinion one of the best of all darts players.

Lew Walker (Kent)

One of the best dart players I have ever seen over a long period of time was Lew Walker. I know that it sounds silly to say that I know someone who was as good as Eric Bristow, John Lowe or Leighton Rees, but without any shadow of doubt this chap was their equal when playing at his best. I suppose up and down the country there are players who when on form are brilliant, but who did not have the breaks like some of today's stars do. Lew was one of these. Now practically retired from the game, although he still plays in a couple of local leagues, Lew is a former Kent player and was once picked as an England reserve. He was never actually picked to play for England, and I think it was their loss. I suppose in all the years I have seen Lew play for Kent he must have lost some games, but I simply cannot remember when.

When Lew was playing at his best he used to make a mockery of the game by being so totally consistent in scoring and so brilliant at finishing.

You are probably wondering why Lew's name is not on many major championship trophies. Well this is because of what I said earlier about certain breaks that one must have to gain any success. It may be determination is also to do with it but whatever it is, Lew did not have his fair share.

He is now in his 50s and way past his best, but still turns in some good performances in the local super league. Lew's style was another good feature. When standing on the oche he was like John Lowe today, slow and methodical. He was also a brilliant counter.

I once saw Lew very nearly do the 9 dart 501 while playing Peter Chapman, the former *News of the World* Champion in the Sussex Open in the mid-1970s. Lew scored: 180, 180 and on his next visit to the board scored treble 20, treble 15 and just narrowly missed the double 18. Lew finished the game on his next trip to the board and completed the game in 11 darts. Every player has their favourites and Lew is one of mine, and I still say quite categorically that Lew was one of the best that I have ever seen.

Chapter Seventeen
The Professionals

There are many stars in our sport who have gained much success, their skill and dedication surprising the world with their consistency in play. I have only included a few of the better players of today and have omitted the majority, simply because I could write forever about all the great players that I know.

John Lowe

Probably the nearest thing you will get to a dart-playing machine is John. His consistency and concentration have helped him become one of the best players of all time. I not only respect him as a player but I admire him for his dedication and total commitment. I first met John in 1975 in Bristol when competing in the Nodor British Open. I had to play John in the last sixteen, and although I won I knew then that this chap was not only good, but if the way he played against me was a sample of his skill, then it would not be long before he was going to make his mark on the dart scene. My assumptions were correct and John has progressed from a relatively unknown county player to a world champion. He has won many major competitions like the World Professional

One of the most familiar figures in the darts world, John Lowe, playing for England. Note the pear-shaped flights which John prefers.

championship, British Open, World Masters, Gold Cup Singles, British Matchplay and British Pentathlon to name but a few. He has been the Captain of the England team.

John not only plays carefully he always dresses carefully and his presentation is second to none. Anybody who wants to get on will certainly help themselves by emulating John. He takes great pride when playing and always plays well. I have seen John beaten of course, but it is not because he played badly, only that his opponent played better. He is very much a method player. He uses pear-shaped flights because they travel through the air quicker and because he only uses three fingers to grip the dart has designed his own barrel. This is very short and enables him to hold the dart in exactly the same place all the time, as it does not give his fingers the chance to move up and down as a normal barrel would. John is a member of the Marlboro Team of Champions.

Leighton Rees

Leighton is definitely a 'Mr Nice Guy'. He hails from the Welsh valleys, is a former storeman and now a top professional. He has won practically everything there is to win and as his career is far from over, who is to say he will not have the few titles which have escaped him under his belt by the time he retires. As the records show, Leighton is more of an invitation tournament player than an open competition player, but that certainly does not mean he is any easier to beat. In opens, where many county players, pub players and professionals compete, it is very hard to play consistently well over a long period of time and the going is very tough, especially if you encounter very good opposition. With invitation tournaments however, the draw is usually made well in advance of the start so everyone knows who he is playing. Leighton is the type of player who welcomes knowing whom he is drawn against, and what he has to do to win. A fantastic scorer who has achieved many maximums on television, Leighton holds the world record for 501, which at the moment is ten darts. His

Former world champion Leighton Rees playing in a Butlins tournament in 1979.

scores were 137, 180, 180, double 2. You can hardly get nearer the magic nine-dart game than that.

Although a big man of about 18 stone he is full of life and agility and is another player who always dresses smartly. I have seen him in action many times at exhibitions and he always gives his best when entertaining an audience.

He is a keen pigeon fancier and I also understand he should never be challenged to a game of table tennis, because he may surprise you a little!

The following he has from the Welsh fans is second to none and when playing in the finals of any major competitions you can be sure that the hall will ring with the sound of Welsh voices. Leighton too is a member of the Marlboro Team of Champions.

Eric Bristow

This chap always seems to take a great deal of harrassment from players and spectators alike. Some say he is arrogant, others say he is even worse, but whatever is said about him there is no getting away from the fact that he is simply one of the world's best. I personally do not like to hear too many people criticise Eric, because I think they are doing him a great injustice. Most of it is only jealousy because they would dearly love to have his ability, confidence and above all, aggressive will to win.

He will always be the first person to tell you that he is the best, and I have even heard him say at the beginning of a tournament that he is going to win. Only rarely is he wrong! Owing to the experience and ability he has for one so young, many people believed that Eric was merely a 'flash in the pan'. Time has, however, proved everybody wrong and Eric still collects major titles quite regularly.

He started playing for England in his teens and has progressed rapidly from there. Eric is always very talkative and never at a loss for words. If you ever play him in a tournament he will undoubtedly talk to you and say something like: 'Hard luck mate' before the game has even begun. To me, this is not really being 'flash' because you in turn, have every right to say the same to him. I think this is just Eric's way to combat nerves. Of course, this type of comment can work for him or against him because it can make his opponent so mad that he plays better than ever or it can reduce him to a complete nervous wreck!

World Professional Champion in 1980 and 1981, Eric is and always will be a winner. Nothing else will ever be good enough. In 1981 he took over the England captaincy.

Bobby George

Bobby is quite a unique character who never seems in a bad mood and always appears to be laughing whether he is winning or losing. Being just another professional darts player was not what Bobby was after so he looked around for a gimmick and found it by wearing outlandish sequinned shirts, earning himself the nickname of 'Liberace'. He is an exceptional player who came late into the

Top: 'The Crafty Cockney' is the name of an American bar, but it has been taken over and made famous by Eric Bristow, world no 1 of the 1980s.

Below: One of the most popular players on the circuit (and one of the best), Bobby George.

53

game, but his skill, especially when winning the 1979 *News of the World* title is something to be admired. Built like a muscle man, he was once a self-employed floor layer and is now something of a D.I.Y. enthusiast, having taken a great deal of time and care to dig and instal the heating system for a swimming pool in his own back garden. He is very fit and can adapt himself to any job whether it be building a house or getting three bulls-eyes on the dart board!

He has what would seem to be a very awkward, unconventional way of throwing, because although he is right handed, he throws from the left side of his face. I myself have often tried this and have so far managed to assassinate two chalkers and one publican!

Bobby's attitude towards life in general is exceptionally good and happy-go-lucky and he would quite easily talk to Fred the Dustman and the Duke of Edinburgh in the same conversation.

The British Darts Organisation Sporting Personality Award for 1980 was given to Bob, and this came as no real surprise to me because he really gets on well with anyone, whether they are 9 or 90.

Alan Glazier

Without a doubt one of the best players I have ever seen is Alan Glazier. In 1975 I saw Alan play a challenge match against a young Swede called Stefan Lord, who would progress into arguably the best foreign player on the circuit today. However, Alan's consistency in this match of one leg of 3,001 astounded me. I have since seen Alan compete in tournaments and television competitions and he has always impressed me.

Left-handed Alan unfortunately has a flaw in his game. He has the ability to beat John Lowe, Eric Bristow, Leighton Rees and Bobby George in a competition and then lose to Cecil Cockroach in the final! This man has reached the finals or final of nearly every major competition only to fall at the last hurdle. There is

Left: Often called 'the world's best left-hander', Alan Glazier has plenty of trophies to prove his prowess.

Right: Tony Brown, with a Kent man-of-the-match award.

really no answer to this, except perhaps Alan should have a brain transplant! Or at the very least a good kicking. If he had reversed all the decisions in which he lost in the final he would always be in the top three or four of the world rankings.

Although Alan has had the misfortune of losing all these titles he has never let it get him down to the point where he considers giving up the game. Obviously disappointments such as Alan has experienced over the years must have affected him the very next time he got into a final, but he has always tried to overcome this and hence produced great darting.

He has, of course, won the North American Open and the Embassy L.V. tournament and is often referred to as the 'Ton Machine' or 'The man in black'.

He has a very good sense of humour and the sort of temperament which you need to continue in this sport. He is a former member of the Marlboro Team of Champions.

Tony Brown

Tony is one of the better England players. In fact John Lowe once said that Tony's name should be the first on any selection sheet. He has turned in memorable performances for England over the past few seasons, the highlight probably being helping England to victory in the 1979 World Cup. He was also one of the four-man team to win the European Cup which was held in Wales in 1980 and in fact won the individual title and became the European Individual Champion by beating Eric Bristow, the reigning World No. 1, in the final by 4 legs to nil.

However, the going has not always been easy for Tony, as he was always something of a runner-up like Alan Glazier. He has lost in the Ladbrokes Matchplay finals twice, the World Masters final and in the grand finals of the *News of the World*.

In his younger days Tony was a bit of an all-round sportsman playing football and cricket. He in fact excelled at cricket and would probably be playing professional cricket for Kent now if it were not for his work commitments earlier on. He was the foreman at a paper mill and used to have difficulty in getting time off from work. However, in March 1977 Tony was selected to play along-side John Lowe and Eric Bristow in the Jubilee Open Triple which ran parallel to the Jubilee Classic. Tony could not get the time off from the mill, so after being there fiteen years he handed in his notice. The Brown, Lowe, Bristow combination won the open triples which helped put him on his way. He and Stefan Lord won the British Open Pairs earlier in 1977 and he has since won the British Open Individual Championship. He completed a fantastic double in 1977 when he won both Pontins individual events at Brean Sands and Prestatyn. He also collected £1,000 for winning the London Elkadart Classic, a feat he repeated in 1979.

Over the past seasons Tony has established himself as a world class player and top professional well respected for his ability and consistency. He is a member of the Marlboro Team of Champions.

Chapter Eighteen
The Female Front

Over the years more and more women have taken to the sport and many have gained much success in major and minor competitions. There is now a points rating system for women which names the World's Top 10. The points are given on pretty much the same basis as the men's but there are not as many major tournaments for them. There are not many smaller competitions for them either, which I think is a shame. I know that women darts players are looked upon as rather inferior by many men, but their hearts are in the game as much as ours.

I have included in this chapter a few of the most consistent players I know and have seen play many times.

Maureen Flowers

Probably the best known lady player and most certainly the reigning World No. 1 is Maureen. One only has to look at the competitions she has won and watch her play to realise why she holds such a position. Maureen started playing darts at a very early age, having been brought up in a pub atmosphere until she herself began to run a pub in the early 1970s. She decided to find out how good she was and entered the N.D.A.G.B. singles in 1975. She did not win but she was runner-up and also won the pairs title. Her career has progressed from there.

In one international match Maureen finished a 501 leg in 14 darts, which I think many men would be proud of. She can certainly hold her own with the men and I can verify this after having played her in the Thames Telethon 1980. After a shaky start in the first leg, Maureen stepped up to the oche requiring 144. I watched as she finished the leg with 60, 60, double 12! She really hit form and I had to play well to beat her 3–2. Her consistency in competitions has won her many titles such as the Pony Ladies' British Darts Championship, the N.D.A.G.B. singles, the Ladbrokes Ladies' singles and many more. She seems to have no difficulty, having placed one dart in the treble twenty, in making the others follow. She really is a first-class lady player.

Linda Batten

I first met Linda in 1979 when I partnered her along with Tony Sontag in a mixed triples event at Denes Holiday Village, Lowestoft, and I am happy to say we won. Since then I have partnered Linda in a couple of mixed pairs competitions here and in the United States and we always seem to do well. She has won many competitions. Her biggest success was winning the British Open singles in 1980 and beating the World No. 1, Maureen Flowers, in the final. Linda played well throughout the competition, and exceptionally well in the final, in fact clinching the match 3–0 with a bulls-eye finish.

She has a nice easy throwing action and has been playing for
about five or six years. Her father worked in a pub in Enfield and
Linda would often practise on the board there. She maintains a
good international record, although at one stage went through a
bad county season. She was winning her international matches and
playing very well indeed but was unfortunately having trouble with
county matches. Eventually she was dropped to the 'B' side. However, when a new season began and she was recalled to the 'A'
side, she played with such determination she won every game of
the season. The reigning World No. 2 she is constantly pushing
Maureen for that No. 1 position.

Sharon Kemp

This young left hander burst onto the darts scene by winning the
British Open pairs with her partner Pauline Marjoram in January
1980. Sharon played superbly throughout this competition and
thus caught the eye of quite a few people.

When younger Sharon played all sports and was particularly
good at table tennis, winning a few East of England titles. She also
played tennis for Suffolk Under-13s. She decided however, that
she could probably do better at darts and focused all her attention
on this sport. For five years she lived in Australia and returned to
Suffolk in 1970. At 15 she started playing in friendly matches and
eventually joined the ladies' super league in Suffolk. She was
chosen to play for the Suffolk 'B' team and she now maintains a
regular 'A' team place. She has been quite successful in competitions – she won the Rothmans 5 in 1 singles 1980, was runner

Maureen Flowers' dart
looks like Concorde as
it takes off on its way
to the treble 20.

Linda Batten, British
Open champion of
1980, a title won with
a bulls-eye finish.

Sharon Kemp, who first attracted notice in 1980 and soon hit the top.

Janet Dewan, a Welsh international with a knack of always doing well in America.

up in the Danish Open 1980, won the British Open Pairs 1980 and also the Coral Mediterranean Open ladies' pairs, 1980. Sharon works as an assistant accountant with a packaging firm in Lowestoft and her Suffolk accent makes you think that she should be milking the cows down on the farm! She has a very good sense of humour and has received a lot of encouragement not only from family and friends but from her Suffolk team mate Lil Coombes. Her one ambition was to play for England and I am glad to say that soon after I finished the manuscript for this book, Sharon was picked for the team.

When 20-year-old Sharon was asked about boyfriends, she said: 'I just don't have the time, darts comes first', which only goes to show how dedicated she is!

Janet Dewan

Another player I have had the pleasure of partnering is Janet Dewan. We played together along with Tony Sontag in the British Open triples event and took the title.

Janet is a very steady player throughout the course of a competition, whether it be singles or pairs or a team event. She always seems to do particularly well in America, where she has won the Santa Monica Open ladies event two years in succession. She is a regular Powys County 'A' player who has a very good international record for Wales.

She was very successful in 1980 at the Pontins Darts Festival at Prestatyn where she won the singles event together with the mixed pairs event partnered by myself. With her Welsh team-mates Sandra Gibb and Betty Hughes she also won the Bass Ladies' Triples for 1980.

Chapter Nineteen
The Organisers

I have often thought to myself that when my darting days are over I would like to be part of the team, for example, in the British Darts Organisation, and turn my hand to organising, but I am put off when I realise just how many hours are put into our sport by the men who run the organisation.

Another off-putting factor that I think is appropriate to mention here is that very few organisers, if any, get much thanks for the work they do. Next time you go to a major tournament consider the amount of work being put into running the tournament smoothly. Many of these organisers have to get up in the very early hours of the morning, go to the venue, set up the boards, put down the oches, fix up all the lighting for the boards and set up all the stage equipment and electronic scoreboard etc. Also, through-out the very long competitions, such as the British Open which is held over three days, the organisers have to be alert at all times to ensure the tournaments run to time. The point I am making is that the job of organising is done purely for the love of darts. There is little reward for the organisers, who often dip into their own pockets to benefit the game.

The majority of the men who organise darts have at one time or another played, or perhaps still do in local leagues etc., but they are not as good as today's professionals and therefore keep in the game by using their skills and knowledge to better advantage. Take for instance Master of Ceremonies Tony Green, himself a Lancashire County player but more widely known through tele-vision either commentating or being the M.C. for a major tourna-ment. I partnered Tony while in America and we had quite a bit of success, and indeed won the Golden Gate Pairs tournament. He is a great player in his own right but perhaps has not quite the skills to make it as a top professional, so he turned his hand to being an M.C. and he is probably the best known in the British Isles.

Another organiser who I certainly know to be a very good player is my own Kent team manager, Sam Hawkins. Sam used to play for Kent, and was captain, and was a formidable player. Having lost his edge over the years he now just plays in the super league. Sam is without a doubt one of the best organisers that I have ever known. At work he is the manager of a sheet metal and ventilating company. At play he is the Kent team manager, Assistant B.D.O. Secretary, Fixture Secretary for the South and Chairman of the England Selection team. Sam is married to Marie, who is captain of the Kent ladies' team and is also the Kent Darts Organisation treasurer.

Sam and his family moved to Blackfen in Kent, in 1958 and for 18 years Sam skippered the Woodman team from Sidcup. He then decided it was time for a change and joined the Golden Arms, Chiselhurst and in one year alone his team won 16 trophies. In 1969 Sam won the Kent Super League when playing for Peckham. Sam played six games for London and then decided to break away to form the Kent side which has over a period of six years produced six international players in Tony Brown, George Simmons, Pat Piper, Lew Walker, Chic Love and myself.

Sam is a very jovial person, always with time to chat. One of his ambitions is to hold the trophy when Kent win the British Darts Organisation Inter-County Championship, and he says he would sooner win that than the *News of the World*, even though the *News of the World* is every man's dream.

Another organiser who is known around the world is Olly Croft. He is the type of chap who on first meeting can seem unapproachable, but after knowing him for quite some time I realise that this is not the case at all. When you see him at competitions he always appears to be rushing around everywhere and you can quite easily pass him without being recognised. This is merely because he is so deep in thought about the events going on around him. He is the General Secretary of the British Darts Organisation and is very lucky that he has a wife like Lorna who is behind him every step of the way. Their involvement with the British Darts Organisation grew so much that it took over half of their home. So Olly had an extension built!

Olly founded the B.D.O. because he saw that top players were not being recognised. He also liked a challenge. Now trips are arranged to different parts of the world and there are many major and minor competitions organised by the B.D.O.

Because of darts, Olly and Lorna normally only spend about three weekends out of 52 at home. Their children, before marrying, have to check with Olly to avoid their wedding dates clashing with darts promotions.

Devoted men who look after the organization of the game around the world, these officials are from South Africa, Australia and USA (Tom Fleetwood, whom some will recognise as an actor in the TV western series 'Bonanza').

Chapter Twenty
Useful Addresses

The World Darts Federation is the international controlling body of darts, and it is made up of the following national controlling bodies:

England
Olly Croft, England Darts Organisation, 2 Pages Lane, London N10 1PS.
Ireland
Louis Donahoe, Irish Darts Organisation, Kings Inn Bar, 42 Bolton Street, Dublin, Ireland.
Scotland
Tom Frost, President, Scottish Darts Association, 17 Struan Drive, Iverkeithing, Fife, Scotland.
Wales
Alan Clarke, Welsh Darts Organisation, Royal Oak Hotel, Henfaes Road, Tenna, Nr. Neath, West Glamorgan.
Australia
A. R. Singleton, The Australian Darts Council Inc., 76 Hampton Circuit, Yarralumla A.C.T. 2600, Australia.
Belgium
Roger Vannoorden, President, Belgian Darts Federation, 14 Beek Straat, 8600 Menen, Belgium.
Bermuda
Michael J. Tavares, Bermuda Darts Organisation, P.O. Box 207, Hamilton 5, Bermuda; Gordon H. Monks, The Sportsman's Ship, Box 1264, Reid Street, Hamilton, Bermuda.
Canada
Ron Steggal, National Darts Association of Canada, P.O. Box 13, Station M, Toronto, Ontario, Canada M6S 5TZ; Len Worrell, 12524 – 126 Street, Edmonton, Alberta, Canada.

Denmark
Preben S. Schultz, Dansk Dart Union, Lundemogen 106, 2670 Greve Strand, Denmark.
Finland
Kari Hintikka, Finnish Darts Union, Jaakarink 10A6, 00150, Helsinki 15, Finland.
France
Federation Francaise de Darts, 142 Rue des Landes, 78400 Chatou, France.
Gibraltar
Gibraltar Darts Association, c/o Odd Fellows Club, 3 Victualling Office Lane, Gibraltar.
Holland
Colin Brown, Nederlandse Darts Bond, Post Box 16290, Den Haag, Hongarenburg 96, Den Haag, Holland.
Hong Kong
Tom Smith, Hong Kong Darts Association, c/o The China Fleet Club, Gloucester Road, Wanchai, Hong Kong.
Japan
Bayard R. Brick, Japan Darts Association, 2-26-22 Denenchofu, Ota-Ku, Tokyo, Japan.
Malta
Louis Florian, Malta Darts Association, St. Rita Luqua Road, Pawla, Malta.
New Zealand
I. M. Frazer, P.O. Box 767, Nelson, New Zealand.
South Africa
The South African Darts Association, Mr. S. N. Bam, 81 Da Gama Street, Strand 7140, Cape Province, South Africa.
Sweden
Kent Seagran, Svenska Darforbundet, Box 137, 772 Ozgrangesberg, Sweden.
U.S.A.
Tom Fleetwood, American Darts Organisation, 13841 Eastbrook Avenue, Bellflower, California, 90706, U.S.A.